For Amy –

Mardav Books

Reno, Nevada

ISBN: 9781980837138

Best Regards

Martin

1

Dedicated with appreciation and thanks
To my dear wife Carol

He was a tall man. His skin was between brown and copper in color and very smooth. In fact, it was too smooth for his eyes. Those eyes. The eyes were set deep in a nest of wrinkles but they were not hidden there. Those eyes. They could never be hidden. They demanded attention. They dominated his face. They dominated the room. He was The Stranger and his eyes reached deep inside you and listened to your thoughts every time he talked to you. His beard was a banner of white wool to further celebrate those magical eyes.

I was sitting in a quiet and seldom used reading room in the old, long since replaced, San Francisco Public Library, main branch. I had been delighted when I first discovered the room and found out it was open to the public. It became my habit, on Thursday afternoons, to go to the library, find a number of books and periodicals I needed for research and then to go to the small room that housed a donated private book collection. There I could write in my notebooks for hours without disturbance.

It was there, on a Thursday, that I looked up and saw the tall man watching me.

"Hello."

His voice was like a bass drum and also like gravel. He spoke with the music of some faraway place. I nodded. My smile, if it was a smile, must have been quizzical.

"I want to meet you."

"Me?"

"Yes, have been watching you many weeks. You are a writer."

"Yes."

I had no idea I was being watched all that time. I felt a chill. I looked at him. His white hair fell loosely over his stained, white collar. He wore a battered black fedora and a black overcoat. The warmth of the late fall San Francisco day seemed of no consequence to him.

"I have been looking for a writer. I am a stranger here. I have something to tell about. I will come

again next Thursday. We will talk."
He reached down and put a
feather on the table next to my
notebook and he turned and
walked away. I watched him go.
When I could no longer see him I
looked at the feather. It was about
six inches long and it had evenly
spaced smudged stripes of dark
brown, dusty white and cinnamon.
I found out later that it was a
fallen feather from an owl. The

Stranger collected such things. He was in love with all of creation and he found a story in even the smallest thing.

The Stranger danced in my mind and my life for many years after that first meeting. His words flowed to me and through me. I will try now to share them with you.

The Stories told by The Stranger

Long ago when the Precious Creation was not yet completed; when there was no division between the waters and the sky, The Sun and the Moon were commanded by the Creator of All Things to join in a dance of joy. For six days and six nights they rolled together. The sky and the lands above the sky and the lands below the sky swayed and shook with their joining. Thunder roared and many flashes of lightning made the days and nights as bright as if The Sun and The Moon had never left their places.

When they were still, on the seventh day, the Creator of all things looked around them. They saw that the dust they had stirred up with their coupling had turned to mud from the great rivers of sweat that ran from their heated bodies. The Creator of all things blessed the great ball of mud and so our Mother, the Earth was born. The abundance of their salty sweat also made the oceans. The sounds of their sighs and groans can still be heard in the winds. When they saw what was created they began to laugh. Their laughter brought music to the world.

From the heat of their passion came the many animal spirits. Among the first of these was Coyote, who because of his cunning and skill earned the honor title of Grandfather Coyote.

After Coyote came Owl, who because of her wisdom and vision earned the honor title of Grandmother Owl.

Among the last to come forth were woman and man. Because of

their need they were given
Grandmother Owl and
Grandfather Coyote to guide
them. Now I will tell the stories I
have learned from a whole world
of Grandmothers and
Grandfathers.

The Stranger tells of great travel.
Many ask where travel is going.
The true answer is "We don't know,
we are not yet there."

If travel is always to a place
then the travel itself is lost. When
we set one foot on the trail, one
journey is already complete. When
every step of the journey is lived by
itself we are part of the Earth and

we see the many visions that are given to us.

Sometimes the vision is a tree or a cloud; sometimes it is ourselves and sometimes it is the other travelers. Thinking only of arriving takes away all the visions. Forgetting to see the trail as it unfolds leads us to being lost. It is the same as keeping the eyes closed while on the journey.

When we are lost while traveling we cannot see familiar places and our hearts become uneasy. Often we must turn back to the place where we started to find our way again. If the travel is inside ourselves and we become lost, we cannot see the image of what we wanted and who we wanted to be. If that happens we become sad and frightened because we see how far from the trail we have wandered and how far we must go to return.

To stop growing is to become lost on the journey of the inside. When we look back we see that our trail has become tangled. Perhaps we are not listening to the voices of our visions. The sound of the drum of power or the rattle of coins may drown out our vision voices and lead us where we do not wish to go.

If you awake on your journey and find you are lost, do not lose hope from seeing how far it is to go back. Remember to live every step. Remember every step is a complete journey. Remember to see the visions that are given to us as gifts with every footfall.

If a Coyote wished to be a stallion or an Owl wished to be an eagle their power would be as small as dust. If an Owl said she was really an eagle and a Coyote said he was really a stallion their blindness would be a trap holding them in one place forever.

When the creatures of the air and earth and water were created none was made perfect. The

Creator of All Things wanted all to walk the long path with room to grow.

We humans are the only creatures of the Creator of All Things who search for perfection in our own images. We see the reflection of ourselves in the surface of a disturbed and rippling lake and we tremble because we do not see perfection there. We forget that we are part of the immense family that walks on the Earth and we are not required to be perfect. We are only required to learn and grow.

If we tremble because we are not the image of perfection we have taught ourselves to expect, we tremble more when we think someone else can see our flaws. If we think someone is about to speak in either an honest tongue or in a mean and painful voice about our blemishes, we become afraid and we become angry. We fear that we will not be liked because of our faults.

If we understand in our hearts that we are children of the Creator of All Things and of Mother Earth then we will permit mistakes. We will not ask ourselves or others to be perfect. We will open the clouds under which we

have hidden and make room so we
can grow to the sky.

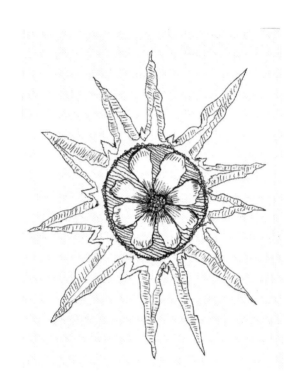

When the spirit of one human and the spirit of another human meet in the place where the winds are silent both spirits are set free. One spirit must not try to control another spirit. They can only rejoice in their meeting and remember to help each other grow.

The joining of two human spirits creates a new spirit that is part of one and part of the other but not completely one or the other. This new spirit is alive and also must grow

If one spirit stands and waits, the new, joined spirit will grow weak and die. Both must give nourishment to the new spirit. Both must give honor to the new spirit.

Helping the new spirit grow must be done if the two human spirits are mates or friends and also if they are parent and child. We must remember that it is the Creator of All Things who guides us into the circle and when we share love with another we can hear the Creator of All Things speaking to us.

Sharing love is like singing prayers to the spirits of the earth and water and sky. Sharing love is like a silent stillness in the forest. Sharing love is also like building a house. Work must be done to raise a roof and work must be done to keep a roof from growing old and welcoming in the rain.

The wise ones have said that to get water one must go to the well with an empty bucket. To gather wisdom or to seek after a spirit vision we must first open ourselves and practice being empty buckets.

The human creature suffers from control disease. Everything must be controlled. We try to put our will into all things. We shape rivers and try to control Mother

Earth. We try to control each other and control our experiences.

When we ask "How can I move closer to the Creator of All Things?" we are not thinking clearly. That question comes from control thinking. The only true answer is to be open, to be an empty bucket. Spiritual messages come our way every minute. If we quiet the power drums and war drums and money rattles in our heads we will receive the wisdom of our surroundings. Then the Creator of All Things will move closer to us.

The same is true for receiving the communication from all the animal spirits and earth spirits and even from Mother Earth herself. If we are empty buckets when we approach them, they will give wisdom and strength.

Even pain gives wisdom in its way. Ugliness teaches about beauty. Darkness teaches us about light. We may learn from the spirit of a storm or from the spirit of a rock. If the heart will be open we can be surprised by what will enter.

A wise person learns to grow in many ways. Eyes must be open and heart must be open. If we see a flower but do not smell it, a spirit message is lost. If we smell a flower but do not hear the wind around us, a spirit message is lost. We must be there with all senses if we wish our journey to have value.

Do our enemies deserve our revenge? When we give revenge we give away great energy. When we think of revenge we use up much of our strength.

When we spend our time dreaming of how we will give wounding blows to those who have

injured us, we are keeping the pain
of our wounds fresh.

If we give the gift of our
greatest energy and our most
powerful visions to our enemies as
we plot retaliation, we will lack
power and strength to give life
gifts to ourselves and to our
friends. We must give our
treasured selves to those who ride
by our sides in times of need.

Our enemies will not diminish, but our friends will grow. If we wait for banners of peace and forgiveness to rise in the camps of our enemies we will be trapped there; waiting. We must make our own peace within ourselves and then move on.

When we receive a wound we can learn its lessons and read its wisdom. Then we can leave it behind and keep traveling up our trail of understanding. If we stay with the wound and the pain we will keep them from healing. If we stay with the pain and the wound we will keep ourselves from moving forward. We must ask ourselves, "Do I enjoy feeling this pain?" If the answer is "no," we must forget the pain and move closer to the next pleasure.

There are many kernels on an ear of corn, but when they are gone, they are gone. There are many days in a human life.

Today is one of my corn kernels. When I have chewed the flavor out of today it will be gone. I am trading my day for something. What do I trade this precious day for?

If I respect my days on earth I will respect that which I trade for this day. Is the Creator of All Things in me when I do my work or is this day's work something I cast away without care? Only I may decide.

Will this day pass forever without my stopping to play? Will trees and birds disappear from this day without my having smiled at their beauty? Only I may decide.

Will I spend some part of this day in worshipping the Creator of All Things within myself? Will I care for myself and seek physical and spiritual nourishment? How much time will I spend alone with the voice that echoes inside my own heart? Will I share some notes from my heart song with the world before this day fades? Only I may decide. Only I may decide.

All things must change; that is the law of the universe. We may know change while we are flying with eagles or while we are standing still. Even the person who takes no risks and challenges no storms still withers and dies. It is only to grow or not to grow that we choose.

A leaf in the autumn may cling to its tree and try to control the change that must come. But we are like the leaves that fall. We cannot know where we will land. We cannot control the direction of the winds that send us on our journey. Part of the joy of our journey is not knowing where we are being taken.

We may cling to our belongings, but we cannot control the lightning bolt or the falling boulder. We may cling to our safety, but we cannot prevent the wind from changing our course. We may cling to our friends and family and loved ones, but we cannot drown out the sound of the forest owl calling their names. All people and things must move on in the path of change.

Even good fortune comes to us without our control. All we can control is how we choose to grow past the moment of change and how we gather wisdom from it. We

can seek the lesson in each thing

and then we have chosen growth.

The Stranger tells of four spirit roads and how they join to guide our travel: The grass road; the deer road; the tree road and the road of the stone.

In the days of Earth's youth, the Creator of All Things called four spirits forth and told them they must take the task of guiding all those who walk upon two feet on the land.

"Sweetgrass, you who move in one life from soft green to glowing gold," the Creator of All Things said, "you must wave forever in a dance with the wind. You may echo the wind's song, but only quietly. It is you who show the path of gentleness. All who walk beneath the sky must learn the way of gentleness and must whisper the gentle song of the wind. So shall it be."

To the deer the Creator of All Things said, "You shall be hunted over the face of Mother Earth. I give you swift motion so you may run from the hunters. But when their arrows find you, you must go with them. For your flesh shall nourish them and their kind. I shall instruct them to honor your spirit and to invite your spirit to join them at their feast. You are the guardian of the deer road and that is the path of sharing. Sharing shall be a law I give to those who live by hunting and you shall teach them to share. So shall it be."

"Tree spirit, you who stand firmly on the face of the earth, you shall show the road of honesty. None shall see your strong roots without remembering to keep their roots deep in the ground of honesty. So shall it be."

To the stone spirit the Creator of All Things spoke with reverence. "Oh grandfather stone spirit, you who are older than all things upon the face of Mother Earth, you shall live forever. You shall be the symbol of the road of strength and wisdom. All who see you shall remember to travel with strength and to seek the path of wisdom. So shall it be."

When all the other spirits, animal spirits, wind spirits, fire spirits, heard of the four roads that were one road, they all asked the Creator of All Things how they too could help.

"Can we not watch the two-legged creatures and tell you when they fall from the sacred road?" they asked.

"Shall we not follow them and nip at their heels when they stray from the path?" some of the animal spirits asked.

"No," said the Creator of All Things, "this shall be a path of choice. All may choose to walk this road. Those who fall from the road are free to return to the road. Those who forget the road may find it again without guilt. My road with four guardians is a road of harmony and when all choose to walk on it, harmony will bless the earth and all creatures."

So shall it be.

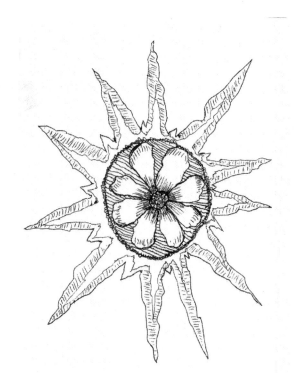

It is easier to lie to oneself or to a whole tribe than it is to lie to one's dog.

If you lie to your dog, the dog will know you are lying. If the dog does not see the lie when you say it, the dog will know the truth in time.

If you tell false words to a whole tribe or to one person, you may succeed in hiding your falseness. That is because people want to believe in the fantasy behind the clouds and whirlwinds of words.

Dogs are not smarter than people, but dogs do not understand fantasy. Dogs see only what is there.

We must invite the dog spirit to live inside of us. If we hear false words spoken—or if we speak false words—we must teach ourselves, like the dog, to see only what is really there. In that way it will be more difficult for others to lie to us and we will master the important skill of telling only the truth to ourselves.

Honesty is important as we grow along our path. If we wish to gather honesty to feed us on our journey we must first see our lies. We must see the lies we have told others. We must see the lies we have told ourselves.

We lie to ourselves when the road of honesty becomes uncomfortable. We give ourselves small lies to cover the sharp places on the road. When the small lies grow thin we add thicker lies. Soon we forget that the lies are not our skin. We forget that the lies are only coverings we have added to hide from our pain.

Each day we must look at one thin lie we have used to cover ourselves and we must put it aside. Soon we will be strong enough to walk over the pointed edges of our honesty and the pain will not frighten us.

Even a blind person can see the suffering of another being and stretch forth a hand of help. Only those who are spirit blind will pass without helping.

If we carry many burdens we sometimes let the sweat run into our eyes and take away our true vision. If we see only the burdens they may become heavier. Soon the world disappears and only the burdens are left.

Look on all sides. Touching those who walk nearby brings healing to our aching spirit. Sharing food with the hungry traveler, even when we ourselves are hungry, will increase the life power of the food. Are the elders around us in need of a voice or a touch? It is in those elders that the wisdom of our past is stored.

We can use that wisdom to walk into our future. When we help another carry life burdens up the mountain, our own burdens can become lighter.

Looking at the needs of another moves our own needs further away from the light of the fire circle.

Touching the needs of others puts a magic spirit on the earth. When you help another and they wish to thank you in some way, do not say, "It is nothing, forget it." Tell them instead that can thank you in a specific way. That way to give back what you have given them—only they must give it to the next person they see who needs their help. In that way you will start a magic circle and the earth will be healed.

Do not dance when it is time to hunt. Do not hunt when it is time to dance. Do not stop to look for small, colored stones when it is necessary to reach shelter before the sun goes down.

The Stranger laughs to hear people ask, "Where did the time go?" Time is not a bucket of water that sometimes splashes over the top, sometimes seeps away through a hole, and *sometimes is swallowed*

in thirsty mouthfuls by a parched

voyager. Time flows without

change. Time goes nowhere; it is

we who move in the river of time.

The Creator of All Things does

not change time for each person.

If we hide from our tasks they

will not be done. If we save all

things for "another time" we may

never see that time come or feel it

pass by.

Two travelers saw a great
carver bring forth animal spirits
from pieces of wood. Both of them
spoke wishes that they could also
work such magic with their knives.

"What season is it?" the carver
asked them.

"Why, of course, it is autumn,"
the travelers replied.

"If you begin to learn the ways
of the wood carver, then in one
year, the harvest moon will return

to light the forest and you will see

your hands and your knives begin

to free the spirits who live inside

the wood. If you do not choose to

study the ways of the carver," the

old wood carver told them, "then

you will not learn them, but the

moon will not care. In one year, the

autumn moon will return to hang

over the earth again. The moon

and the sun will continue to dance

in the sky no matter whether you choose to learn carving or not."

The words of the carver are true. The river of time flows steadily and we must decide how we wish to swim in that river.

Do not deny anger. Do not deny the rain. Both rain and anger will come. Even people whose love leads them to travel forever on the same road will experience anger between them.

When we feel pain, and our fear tells us it will not go away, we often slide over to the bitter pools of anger. Because our love is strong, our hurt is great, and our anger is deep.

When we feel anger we must acknowledge it. We need to tell ourselves that we can be angry and still continue to love. Our frustration and pain do not have to lead us to close the door of our love. Anger is not the same as hatred. We should not feel ashamed when our euphoric feelings of love are interrupted by anger. A love without a variety of feelings is a love without passion.

So what must we do when anger grows within us? We know what to do when we feel rain. We prepare for rain by purchasing an umbrella and carrying it. We must prepare for anger too. Fairness and honesty are our umbrellas when warm drops of anger fall into our love. It is not shameful to fight with our friends and our loved ones. It is only shameful to fight unfairly and to be cruel. We have the right to feel anger, but we never have the right to be cruel.

When we fail to feel our hurt and our fear, we go easily into anger. When we deny our anger, we no longer have control of it. When we give up that control, we no longer are fair or honest. We say things that cause deep damage between us and our closest soul mates. If we admit our waves of anger and admit our unfairness, we can move beyond that hurt. If we feel and admit where we have been, we can move along the road to new places. We can repair the damage we have done and learn to change our reaction to our hurts.

The Stranger speaks of the difference between paint and a house. That which we see as permanent may be temporary, but our wishes cannot make the temporary things stay forever.

A house may be green and a house may be brown. The same house may be white and then may be green again or even green and brown and white at the same time.

A house may be made of wood. It will always be made of wood. A house may be made of brick. It will always be a brick house.

We must know what things are forever and what things can be changed. If we forget to see the difference, we may fool ourselves into keeping things that we should change. Our minds and hearts sometimes listen to our voices and are fooled.

If we are feeling sad, our sadness is like a color on the outside of our house. It can be changed. If it is held on to, it may be changed to very dark sadness. That sadness is depression and it becomes difficult to imagine such a dark stain ever leaving our lives. If we understand that the sadness is a feeling—a color that can easily be changed—we can let it go. Letting go of a feeling can allow that feeling to visit and then move on.

Saying, "I am depressed," may tell the mind and heart that sadness and depression are permanent states. It is better to say, "I am feeling depressed." A feeling is something that visits and then leaves. Recognizing temporary feelings and calling them by their names helps them continue their journeys.

Even joy is a feeling that may stay with us a while and then proceed again. Holding on to our feelings and denying their movement will not allow us to grow. If we demand that our feelings stay with us and never change, we will be frightened and disappointed when they leave. If we succeed in holding them, they will change and we will change. We will be cut off from our own inner visions and it will be the feelings that hold us instead of our holding our feelings.

I am a man. I am a woman. I am tall. I am short. These are the wood and brick of our being. These are to be accepted—just as the color of the paint is to be changed. I am angry. I am unhappy. These are the paint that can be changed while the house itself remains the same.

Why do you run from childhood and then back to childhood, The Stranger asks?

In places where there is great need, the children are forced to be adults. Children must help provide the means for the family to survive. They often must go out on their own and exist in a hostile world—with no thought of childish things.

However, in times and places where there is plenty; where the meager contribution of tiny hands is not a necessity, children rush to become adults. They act as if they are ashamed to be children and as if childhood were a state of imprisonment. They break all rules and social boundaries in their rush to be like adults, and then to be adults.

Is it boring to be a child? Do we make our children think it is better and safer to be an adult? That seems to be the case. The children seem to think so. At least they think so while they are children.

As adults we learn another way. We who ran from our childhood as if it were strangling us suddenly realize that it is adulthood we should have been avoiding. How quickly we become bored with the state of adulthood we once sought so anxiously. Now our great struggle, our longing and our goal is to be as children again. To play and laugh like children. To look for all that we lost as children. We try to see with the eye of the child and hear with the ear of the child. We strain to listen to the voice of the child we feel is trapped inside of us. If our inner child is trapped it is because that child was not allowed to be completed. For so many reasons we have jumped over all or part of our childhood and the child who was once us has never grown to completion.

The child inside of us must live and grow. We must seek the counsel of that youthful self just as we seek the counsel of the elder within us.

And what of the real children? They need to learn from our respect and from our eyes and hearts that being a child is a good thing. The must learn that childhood is a rare gift—not something to run away from.

If there is one folly shared by all, The Stranger observes, it is the folly of the hunt for gold. Both wise sages and fools leave themselves behind and join the wild pursuit—even if it kills them.

The practitioners of healing are kept busy around the calendar and around the clock repairing humans who have broken themselves while trying to find gold. It is a circle that needs to be ended.

How sad that any one of us would sacrifice our pleasure and sacrifice our time to be with people we love—just to earn more money. The gold we gain may be necessary. We cannot have sustenance and we cannot have shelter without it. But our quest sometimes goes beyond the basic need itself. The quest itself becomes a goal. We lose sight of our needs and the gold itself becomes a need. We lose sight of our pleasure. We lose sight of friends and family.

Is it possible to be of this world and yet to avoid the race for the gold? It is possible. It is difficult, but it is possible. When we are in the race, we run so far ahead or ourselves that we no longer see ourselves. The body and the mind are no longer respected or nourished. We may gain our golden goal, but health is sacrificed. That is when we attend the circle of healers. We beg them to help us. We offer them everything to give us back that which we have thrown away. They demand—and we offer them— everything we have worked for.

We have lost our health in order to gain gold and we must

give away our gold to ransom back our health. It is a dance that makes no sense. It is a dance we must leave behind. We must dance with our minds and hearts among the stars. If we gain wisdom, we will see that our gold is not able to help us buy back life.

The Stranger tells that one of life's most important lessons is to learn that a truly rich person is not the one who has the most, but is one who needs the least.

So much has been said about the wealthy person who is sad and about the burdens that fall on the shoulders of those who have amassed great fortunes. These stories sound preposterous to those who are suffering in poverty or who live in fear of the consequences of their lack of means. It is difficult to believe the stories. They seem like tales invented to soothe those who are struggling to meet even the simplest level of comfort. Sometimes this is true. History presents many reasons to fear the righteous anger of those who are poor and unfairly treated. The rich

and the poor often have one thing
in common. That one thing is
dissatisfaction. Having great stores
of wealth and great accumulation
of goods ceases to be a source of
pleasure when dissatisfaction steps
in. Emptiness of spirit cannot be
filled with material goods. The
voyager who keeps moving the goal
higher and higher up the mountain
of desire will never know the
healing rest and comfort of

pausing at the top and embracing life. The truest and most lasting pleasure is that which comes from inner peace. There is no predetermined level to which a person must strive. The modest soul who lives in a state of balance has no needs beyond those that are already met is truly in possession of great wealth. The wealthy being who is surrounded by expensive things and takes great pleasure in every belonging without feeling the burning need to strive for more is richer than most of us could dream of.

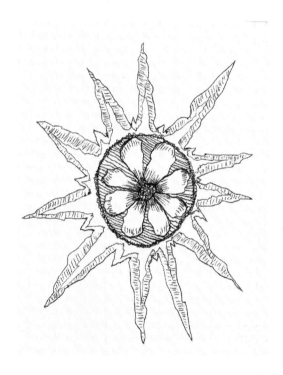

The Stranger tells of the time someone came to the woods and drew a line. The foolish chipmunks came and saw the line and cried, "There is a barrier in the forest. We cannot cross over." The bear came and saw the line and complained, "It is not straight enough." The coyote came and saw the line and said, "It is a path. I can use it to find new places. I will walk in my own steps, but I can always come back to the path and find my way." The owl flew high over the forest and said of the line, "It is good. It is a connection between all that has been and all that is now. If we hold on to the line, we will come to all that will be without losing our bond to what has come before."

I want to speak of threads, said The Stranger. Threads can tie us so we may not move. They can divide things from each other and create obstructions to the free movement of the mind. The simple strength of a thread can be magnified until it is used to enforce rigid rules. But a thread may also serve as the connection that gives guidance and shape to our paths. We all live in a world of time. We were all born in the past. We live in a moment called *now* and we will die in a time called the future. We all belong to something called time. When we try to deny this reality of time, we are letting go of this thread. Part of our past is our teachers. There have been times when people found all lines, all paths, all threads, all rules oppressive. They proclaimed a life without rules. They decided upon a life without discipline. All old paths were abandoned and only new paths were respected. The old paths are the paths of my elders, they cried. The ways of my teachers are the old ways. I must be independent of all that, they proclaimed. I must have no influences. I must have no ties to how things were done in the past. I must listen to no voices but my own. The spirit that led to this rebellion was good, but when the dancers in the street cut the lines to their past, they lost the wisdom of their teachers. That was a time of sadness, for the teachers were part of a thread that stretched back into the histories of many lives. The strands woven by the teachers, the discipline of the teachers were not barriers. They were not restrictions. The way of the teachers are the ways of the spirit guides. These guides do not enforce their wills. They open doors and show us roads. Their lines are the lines of the coyote who walks in his own steps, but knows how to find himself in time. They are the lines of the owl, connecting past to present to future and connecting us to the strength of the earth.

The Stranger tells of two wanderers who view the same oasis.

The desert is hot and many travelers set out to voyage across its shifting sands. There are many destinations and many starting points. Even the most lightly packed wanderer carries an invisible load of stories. Each of us carries on our shoulders the stories of our own lives.

So it was that two such travelers arrived at the same oasis in the desert at the same time and from opposite directions. They exchanged the customary greetings and sat down to enjoy the cool shade and the flowing waters. They filled their water jugs and relaxed from their wearying journey.

"There is welcome comfort here," one of them said, as he stretched out and felt the refreshing breezes that wafted among the trees.

"Oh, it is still much too warm," replied the other.

"Perhaps," said the first, "but the trees here will shelter us and provide us with fresh dates and other edibles."

"There is nothing here that I can eat," complained the other traveler. "Besides, the water that flows here might be tainted. I'll probably have to empty my jug in the middle of the desert and endure thirst until I reach the city."

"I have met many on the path who praise the sweetness of the waters here."

"Well, travelers lie and exaggerate. They are not to be trusted."

And so it was for the time the two travelers rested. One of them breathed in the comfort of the haven in the midst of the challenging desert and the other grumbled over every part of the experience. When it was time to bid farewell to each other and travel on, one was rested and the other was uncomfortable and weary.

They had been in the same shelter and they would be facing the same kind of difficulties on their remaining journey. However, each of them carried on his shoulders the weight of his own story. The experiences we face may be similar, but the way we choose to view them and interpret them is what makes up the narrative of

our lives.

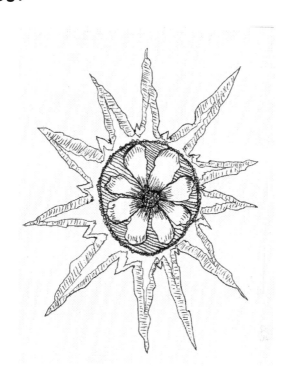

The Stranger tells of a passionate friendship that almost died. A true friendship is like a delicate plant that sprouts slowly and softly, but can become a sturdy and noble tree. A sharp axe, no matter how small it is, may make a wound in the tree. "Oh yes," The Stranger said, "the wound will heal, but if you wander in the forest, you will see the scars that remain on many large trees."

The fox and the raccoon were deepest friends. All the creatures of the woods knew of their friendship and were inspired by it. They often travelled together. When each of them went their own way in the great woods that are as old as the creation of the world, they would always meet at the end of long journeys and share stories, camaraderie, and treasures. That is why that which happened on a day when the wind sent chills through the thickest fur, and the angry-looking dark clouds tried to hide the sunlight shocked all the other animals.

What they all learned on that sad day was that it only takes a few seconds to open profound wounds in persons we love and that it can take many years to heal them. The fox and the raccoon knew each other's secrets—both the good secrets and also the not so good ones—they never spoke of these things and they never shared them with any of the others. After all, a true friend is someone who knows everything about you and likes you anyway. The unhappy happening was during the season when the leaves fall and the trees shiver in anticipation of winter. The two good friends had been apart for a

full passage of the moon and
rejoiced to see each other again.
They were excited to share the
stories of what they had seen in
their travels. Raccoon and fox
began speaking at once. Then they
laughed and each one told the
other to begin first. Finally, they
decided fox would begin. He told
of seeing a huge hill with water
cascading down one side like a

shower of diamonds in the sunlight.

"Oh," said raccoon, "that is nothing compared to the crashing ocean waves I saw on the coast."

"Wait, I am not finished," said fox.

"Yes, but I need to tell you."

"Your turn will come, but now I am speaking. You are always interrupting me. You and your kind are so rude," snapped the fox.

"Well, I may be rude," said the raccoon, "but at least I am not a thief. I remember that egg you stole."

The fox became silent with humiliation. It was true that once, when he was very young and foolish, he had stolen an egg from the nest of one of the forest birds. It was a bad thing to do, but he had done it more out of youthful curiosity than out of meanness. In the years since that time, he had grown to be a much more responsible and thoughtful creature.

"I see," said the fox, and he turned and disappeared into the shadows.

Those that saw him said there were tears flowing from his eyes. It was a long long time before the forest creatures saw the two friends together again. When they did reconnect, there was less joy between them. Of course there was forgiveness because no matter how good a friend is, they're going to hurt you every once in a while and you must forgive them for that.

Like the tall trees in the forest, the friendship between the raccoon and the fox survived and continued to grow. However, like trees that have been marked with an axe, there was a small scar that remained.

"Keep in mind," The Stranger said, "People will forget what you said. People will forget what you did, but people will never forget how you made them feel."

These are some of the stories and observations The Stranger shared with me. There are many others, and I may tell them at another time.